Contemporary Cushions

Contents

Welcome

Knitted cushions are gorgeous to snuggle up with in your home plus they make fantastic presents for friends and family. Whether you're updating your home with this year's colours in simple designs or tackling a more complex pattern, we hope you'll find both inspiration and cool new ideas in this book.

Remember to look out for the stitch library, step-by-step instructions and knitting school tutorials throughout the book.

You can get started on your chunky throw by knitting your first square - it's a very simple double moss stitch square that both knits up quickly and looks really great.

Bright & Easy

○ These cushions in simple knit and purl combinations provide an easy way to update any room. They're simple to knit and cost a fraction of what you'd pay for them in a trendy interiors shop!

Measurements

Pink cushion – 50 x 50cm
Yellow cushion – 45 x 45cm
Orange cushion – 30 x 30cm
Green cushion – 30 x 30cm
Blue cushion – 40 x 30cm

Materials

HOW MUCH YARN

Pink cushion – 7 x 50g balls of Rooster Almerino Aran in colour A – Brighton Rock (shade 307) and 1 ball in colour B – Coral (shade 318)

Yellow cushion – 6 x 50g balls of Rooster Almerino Aran in Custard (shade 305)

Orange cushion – 4 x 50g balls of Rooster Almerino Aran in Coral (shade 318)

Green cushion – 4 x 50g balls of Rooster Almerino Aran in Gooseberry (shade 306)

Blue cushion – 4 x 50g balls of Rooster Almerino Aran in Lagoon (shade 316)

NEEDLES

Pair of 4.5mm (no. 7) knitting needles
Pair of 5mm (no. 6) knitting needles

ADDITIONAL ITEMS

5 buttons (for each of pink and orange cushions)
1 x 38mm self-cover button (for green cushion)
Cushion pads in sizes to match

Tension

Pink cushion – 21 sts and 25 rows measure 10cm square over rib patt on 5mm (no. 6) needles

Yellow cushion – 16 sts and 24 rows measure 10cm square over textured patt on 5mm (no. 6) needles

Orange cushion – 19 sts and 30 rows measure 10cm square over textured patt on 5mm (no. 6) needles

Green and blue cushions – 19 sts and 24 rows measure 10cm square over st st on 5mm (no. 6) needles

IT IS ESSENTIAL TO WORK TO THE STATED TENSION TO ACHIEVE SUCCESS

Pink cushion

FRONT

Using 5mm (no. 6) needles and A, cast on 107 sts.

1st row: (RS) K2, *p1, k1, p1, k2, rep from * to end.

2nd row: P3, *k1, p4, rep from * to last 4 sts, k1, p3.

These 2 rows form rib patt. Rep them until work measures 45cm from beg, ending with a WS row.

Change to 4.5mm (no. 7) needles. Join in B.

With B, work 2 rows in patt. Cut off B. With A, work 4 more rows.

1st buttonhole row: (RS) (K2, p1, k1, p1) twice, *k2, p1, yrn, p2tog, (k2, p1, k1, p1) 3 times, rep from * 3 more times, k2, p1, yrn, p2tog, (k2, p1, k1, p1) twice, k2.

Work 4 more rows in patt. Cut off A.

Join in B, work 2 rows, ending with a RS row. Cast off in patt.

BACK

Using 5mm (no. 6) needles and A, cast on 107 sts. Cont in patt as given for Front until work measures 55cm from beg, ending with a WS row. Cast off in patt.

Making up

Pin out pieces to measurements, cover with damp cloths and leave until dry. With Front and Back RS together, line up cast-on edges. Fold down top 5cm of Back, sandwiching top 5cm of Front between. Pin, then backstitch around three edges. Turn RS out. Sew buttons on to flap to correspond with buttonholes.

Yellow cushion

FRONT

Using 5mm (no. 6) needles cast on 75 sts.

1st row: (RS) K1, (p1, k3) to last 2 sts, p1, k1.

2nd row: P2, (k1, p1) to last st, p1.

3rd row: K3, (p1, k3) to end.

4th row: As 2nd.

These 4 rows form patt. Rep them until work measures 30cm from beg, ending with a WS row. Cast off in patt.

BACK AND FLAP

Work as given for Front until work measures 75cm, ending with a WS row. Cast off in pattern.

Making up

Pin out pieces to measurements, cover with damp cloths and leave to dry. Place Back RS up on a flat surface with cast-off edge at bottom. Lay Front on top, RS down, lining up cast-off edges and folding down top flap of Back to overlap Front by 15cm. Pin, then backstitch together around three edges. Turn RS out.

Orange cushion

FRONT

First piece: Using 5mm (no. 6) needles cast on 59 sts.

1st row: (RS) K to end.

2nd row: P3, (k1, p3) to end.

3rd and 4th rows: K to end.

These 4 rows form patt. Rep them until work measures 17cm, ending with a 4th row. Change to 4.5mm (no. 7) needles.

1st rib row: K3, (p1, k3) to end.

2nd rib row: P3, (k1, p3) to end.

Work 5 more rows in rib as set. Cast off in rib.

Second piece: Using 4.5mm (no. 7) needles cast on 59 sts. Work 4 rows in rib as given for First piece.

Buttonhole row: *K3, p1, k1, yfwd, k2tog, p1, k3, p1, rep from * to last 11 sts, k3, p1, k1, yfwd, k2tog, p1, k3.

Work 4 more rows in rib.

Change to 5mm (no. 6) needles.

Next row: (WS) K to end.

Cont in patt as given for First side until work measures 13cm, ending with a WS row. Cast off.

BACK

Using 5mm (no. 6) needles cast on 59 sts. Cont in patt as given for First piece of Front until work measures 30cm from beg, ending with a WS row. Cast off.

Making up

Pin out pieces to measurements, cover with damp cloths and leave until dry. Place Back RS up on a flat surface. Lay Second front piece on top, RS down, lining up cast-off edges. Lay First front piece on top, RS down, lining up cast-on edges and overlapping ribbed bands. Pin, then backstitch together around all four edges. Turn RS out. Sew buttons on to band to correspond with buttonholes.

Green cushion

FRONT

Using 5mm (no. 6) needles cast on 59 sts. Beg with a k row, cont in st st until work measures 10cm from beg, ending with a p row.

Beg with a p row, cont in reverse st st until work measures 20cm from beg, ending with a k row.

Beg with a k row, cont in st st until work measures 30cm from beg, ending with a p row. Cast off.

BACK

First piece: Using 5mm (no. 6) needles cast on 59 sts. Beg with a k row, cont in st st until work measures 20cm from beg, ending with a p row. Cast off.

Second piece: Using 5mm (no. 6) needles cast on 59 sts. Beg with a p row, cont in reverse st st until work measures 10cm from beg, ending with a k row.

Beg with a k row, cont in st st until work measures 20cm from beg, ending with a p row. Cast off.

BUTTON COVER

Using 5mm (no. 6) needles cast on 13 sts. Beg with a k row, work 6cm in st st, ending with a p row. Cast off.

Making up

Pin out pieces to measurements, cover with damp cloths and leave until dry. Place Front RS up. Lay Second back piece on top, RS down, lining up cast-off edges. Lay First back piece on top, RS down, lining up cast-on edges and overlapping them in centre. Pin, then backstitch together around all four edges. Turn RS out. Following manufacturer's instructions, cover button with knitted square and sew to centre of Front.

Blue cushion

FRONT

Using 5mm (no. 6) needles cast on 78 sts.

1st row: (RS) K39, p39.

Rep this row until work measures 15cm from beg, ending with a WS row.

Next row: P39, k39.

Rep this row until work measures 30cm from beg, ending with a WS row. Cast off in patt.

BACK

First piece: Using 5mm (no. 6) needles cast on 58 sts. Beg with a k row, cont in st st until work measures 15cm, ending with a p row.

Beg with a p row, cont in reverse st st until work measures 30cm from beg, ending with a k row. Cast off.

Second piece: Using 5mm (no. 6) needles cast on 39 sts. Beg with a p row, cont in reverse st st until work measures 15cm from beg, ending with a k row.

Beg with a k row, cont in st st until work measures 30cm from beg, ending with a p row. Cast off.

Making up

Pin out pieces to measurements, cover with damp cloths and leave until dry. Place Front RS up. Lay Second back piece on top, RS down, lining up cast-off edges, cast-on edges and right-hand edges. Lay First back piece on top, RS down, lining up cast-off edge, cast-on edges and left-hand edges with two pieces overlapping in centre. Pin, backstitch around all four edges.

Turn RS out.

Pretty in Pink

○ Perfect for those girly moments, this stocking stitch cushion has a pretty ribbon and bead-trimmed heart stitched on the front.

Measurements

Cushion measures 36 x 36cm

Materials

HOW MUCH YARN

4 x 50g balls of Debbie Bliss Rialto DK in A – Pink (shade 42)

1 ball in contrast colour

 B – Fuchsia (shade 34)

NEEDLES

Pair of 3.75mm (no. 9) needles

Pair of 4mm (no. 8) needles

ADDITIONAL ITEMS

Approximately 125 small pearl beads

1.3 metres of 8mm-wide satin ribbon

Sewing needle and matching thread for sewing on beads

36cm square cushion pad

Tension

With yarn A, 22 sts and 30 rows measure 10cm square over st st on 4mm (no. 8) needles

IT IS ESSENTIAL TO WORK TO THE STATED TENSION TO ACHIEVE SUCCESS

Cushion front

With 4mm (no. 8) needles and A, cast on 81 sts. Beg with a k row, cont in st st until work measures 38cm from beg, ending with a p row. Cast off.

Cushion back

Work as given for Front.

Heart

FIRST SIDE

With 3.75mm (no. 9) needles and B, cast on 8 sts and work from top of heart down.

P 1 row, K 1 row and p 1 row, casting on 3 sts at beg of each row. 14 sts.

Next row: (K1, k1 tbl) into next st, k to last 2 sts, (k1, k1 tbl) into next st, k1.

Next row: (P1, p1 tbl) into next st, p to last 2 sts, (p1, p1 tbl) into next st, p1.

Rep last 2 rows once, then work first row again.

24 sts. P 1 row.

Next row: (K1, k1 tbl) into next st, k to last 2 sts, (k1, k1 tbl) into next st, k1. 26 sts.

Work 3 rows in st st.** Cut off yarn and leave these sts on the needle.

SECOND SIDE

With other 3.75mm (no. 9) needle and B, cast on 8 sts and work as given for first side to **.

JOIN PIECES

Next row: (K1, k1 tbl) into next st, k24, (k1, k1 tbl) into next st, then with RS facing, k across 24 sts of first side, (k1, k1 tbl) into next st, k1. 55 sts.

Work 17 rows in st st, ending with a p row.

Next row: K2tog tbl, k to last 2 sts, k2tog.

Work 5 rows in st st.

Next row: K2tog tbl, k to last 2 sts, k2tog.

Work 3 rows in st st.

Next row: K2tog tbl, k to last 2 sts, k2tog.

P 1 row. Rep last 2 rows to 29 sts, ending with a k row.

Next row: P2tog, p to last 2 sts, p2tog tbl.

Next row: K2tog tbl, k to last 2 sts, k2tog.

Rep last 2 rows to 3 sts, ending with a p row.

Next row: Sl 1, k2tog, psso.

Fasten off.

Making up

Press pieces according to directions on ball bands.

Using the photograph as a guide, thread ribbon around heart, about three stitches in from the edge. Making sure it is centralised, sew heart on to cushion front with a slipstitch using yarn B. Sew beads on to edge of heart using sewing thread and spacing them about 1cm apart. With RS facing, join cushion front and back around three sides with backstitch. Turn right side out. Insert cushion pad and neatly slipstitch opening closed.

Multicolour Stripes

○ Knitted in a smooth aran yarn, the colourful garter-stitch stripes of this cushion contrast with the subtle shade of the stocking stitch background.

Measurements

Cushion measures 40cm square

Materials

HOW MUCH YARN

4 x 50g balls of King Cole Merino Blend Aran in colour A – Aubergine (shade 773)

1 ball in each of three other colours: B – Rose (shade 899); C – Denim (shade 778) and D – Parchment (shade 857)

NEEDLES

Pair of 4mm (no. 8) needles

Pair of 4.5mm (no. 7) needles

ADDITIONAL ITEMS

Cushion pad, 40cm square, 7 buttons

Tension

19 sts and 26 rows measure 10cm square over st st on 4.5mm (no. 7) needles

IT IS ESSENTIAL TO WORK TO THE STATED TENSION TO ACHIEVE SUCCESS

Cushion cover *(worked in one piece)*

With 4mm (no. 8) needles and A, cast on 73 sts.

1st row: (RS) P1, (k1, p1) to end.

2nd row: K1, (p1, k1) to end.

These 2 rows form rib. Work 4 more rows in rib.

Buttonhole row: Rib 6, (yfwd, k2tog, rib 8) 6 times, yfwd, k2tog, rib 5.

Work 5 more rows in rib.

Change to 4.5mm (no. 7) needles.

Joining in and cutting off colours as required, cont in patt as foll:

1st row: (RS) Using B, k to end.

2nd–4th rows: Using B, k to end.

5th row: Using A, k to end.

6th row: Using A, p to end.

7th–16th rows: Rep 5th and 6th rows 5 times more.

These 16 rows form stripe patt.

Cont in stripe patt, working stripes in colours as foll:

C
D
D
C
B
D
C
B
D
D
B
C
D

When last stripe in D has been completed, ending with a ws row, cont as foll:

Change to 4mm (no. 8) needles.

Cont in A only, k 1 row.

Then, beg with 2nd row and omitting buttonholes, work 11 rows in rib.

Cast off evenly in rib.

Making up

Do not press. With RS facing, overlap ribbed sections with button border uppermost. Fold cushion, positioning ribbed borders just below centre back. Join side seams. Turn RS out. Sew on buttons. Insert cushion pad.

Knit Stitch

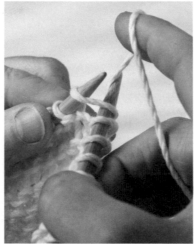

1 The first step is to put the needle in. Insert the point of the right-hand needle in the stitch on the left-hand needle, from front to back.

2 Use your index finger to take the yarn that is attached to the ball around and under the point of the right-hand needle.

3 Draw this new loop on the right-hand needle under and through the first loop on the left-hand needle.

Knit stitch, or garter stitch as the knitted fabric is known, is the simplest stitch of all. It is the first stitch most people learn and is invaluable for a whole range of projects in the Big & Little Knitting Projects.

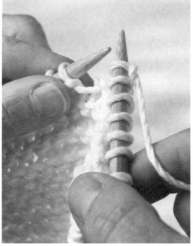

④ This forms a stitch on the right-hand needle. At the same time, slide the original stitch off the left-hand needle.

⑤ You now have a new stitch on the right-hand needle and are ready to make the next stitch by repeating these steps.

⑥ Complete the row of stitches, keeping the tension as even as possible. Now all the stitches on the left-hand needle will have been transferred to the right-hand needle. Swap the right-hand needle into your left hand and begin the next row in exactly the same way.

Rows of knit stitch will look like this, forming a garter stitch pattern with horizontal rows of interlocking stitches.

A Place in the Sun

○ Based on jaunty deckchair stripes and worked in a soft aran cotton yarn, this long, large cushion is a perfect companion for relaxing in the garden.

Measurements

Fits standard size pillow 68 x 46cm

Materials

HOW MUCH YARN

3 x 50g balls of Debbie Bliss Eco Aran in A – orange (shade 601)
5 x balls in B – bright pink (shade 624)
2 x balls in C – blue (shade 615)
1 x ball in D – green (shade 620)

NEEDLES

Pair of 4.5mm (no. 7) knitting needles

ADDITIONAL ITEMS

Stitch markers, 4 large buttons
68 x 46cm pillow pad

Tension

18 sts and 24 rows measure 10cm square over st st on 4.5mm (no. 7) needles

IT IS ESSENTIAL TO WORK TO THE STATED TENSION TO ACHIEVE SUCCESS

Cushion cover *(worked in one piece)*

With 4.5mm (no. 7) needles and A, cast on 83sts.

1st row: (RS) k1, (p1, k1) to end.

Rep this row to form moss st until work measures 8cm from beg, ending with a RS row. P1 row.

Cut off A and join in B. Beg with a k row, cont in st st and stripe sequence of 10 rows B, 2 rows C, 2 rows B, 2 rows D, 4 rows C and 2 rows A, cutting off and joining in colours as required. (Darning in ends after each stripe sequence is recommended.) Rep these 22 rows 4 times more.

Cont in st st, work 20 rows in B, placing markers at each end of 10th row, then reverse stripe sequence as foll: work 2 rows A, 4 rows C, 2 rows D, 2 rows B, 2 rows C and 10 rows B. Rep last 22 rows 6 times more, ending with a WS row.

Cut off B and join in A. K1 row. Cont in moss st for 14cm, ending with a WS row.

1st buttonhole row: (RS) Patt 6 sts, cast off next 3 sts, (patt 20 sts including st used to cast off, cast off next 3 sts) 3 times, patt to end.

2nd buttonhole row: Patt to end, casting on 3 sts over those cast off in previous row.

Work a further 4cm in moss st. Cast off in moss st.

Making up

Avoiding moss st sections, press according to directions on ball band. Place strip of knitted fabric WS down with stripes running vertically and wider moss st band at left-hand edge. Fold over wider moss st band (with buttonholes) on to RS of strip, then fold over right-hand edge of strip at markers so that stripes match at side seams and narrow moss st band overlaps wider one for 8cm. Pin side seams and sew in place, working through all three thicknesses at overlap. Turn cover RS out and sew on buttons to under section of moss st band to correspond with buttonholes. Insert pillow pad and button cover closed.

Jewel Box Bolster

Measurements

46cm long x 20cm in diameter

Materials

HOW MUCH YARN

2 x 50g balls of Debbie Bliss
Prima in each of three colours:
A – turquoise (shade 21)
B – lime (shade 33)
C – red (shade 06)

1 x 50g ball of Debbie Bliss
Cashmerino DK in colour
D – plum (shade 32)

1 x 50g ball of Debbie Bliss Prima in
colour E – bright pink (shade 37)

NEEDLES

Pair of 3.25mm (no.10) needles

Pair of 4mm (no.8) needles

ADDITIONAL ITEMS

4.00mm (no. 8) crochet hook

35cm zip fastener

2 x 38mm buttons for covering

46 x 20cm-diameter bolster
cushion pad

○ Put your feet up and lean back
on this colourful bolster cushion
adorned with fun and funky
bobbles.

Tension

22 sts and 30 rows measure 10cm
square over st st on 4mm (no. 8)
needles

IT IS ESSENTIAL TO WORK TO THE
STATED TENSION TO ACHIEVE
SUCCESS

Cushion main piece

With 4mm (no. 8) needles and D, cast on 152 sts.

Beg with a k row, work 4 rows in st st. Cont in st st and stripes of 4 rows each C and E.

Change to A and work 8 rows.

PLACE BOBBLES

Next row: (RS) With A, k20, mb in C, k21, mb in D, k21, mb in E, k21, mb in B, k21, mb in C, k21, mb in D, k21.

Beg with a p row, work 11 rows in st st.

Next row: (RS) With A, k9, mb in E, k21, mb in B, k21, mb in C, k21, mb in D, k21, mb in E, k21, mb in B, k21, mb in C, k10.

Beg with a p row, work 11 rows in st st.

Next row: (RS) With A, k20, mb in D, k21, mb in E, k21, mb in B, k21, mb in C, k21, mb in D, k21, mb in E, k21.

Beg with a p row, work 11 rows in st st.

Next row: (RS) With A, k9, mb in B, k21, mb in C, k21, mb in D, k21, mb in E, k21, mb in B, k21, mb in C, k21, mb in D, k10.

Beg with a p row, work 7 rows in st st.

Cont in st st and stripes of 4 rows each D, E and C. Change to B and work 8 rows.

PLACE BOBBLES

Next row: (RS) With B, k20, mb in C, k21, mb in D, k21, mb in E, k21, mb in A, k21, mb in C, k21, mb in D, k21.

Beg with a p row, work 11 rows in st st.

Next row: (RS) With B, k9, mb in E, k21, mb in A, k21, mb in C, k21, mb in D, k21, mb in E, k21, mb in A, k21, mb in C, k10.

Beg with a p row, work 11 rows in st st.

Next row: (RS) With B, k20, mb in D, k21, mb in E, k21, mb in A, k21, mb in C, k21, mb in D, k21, mb in E, k21.

Beg with a p row, work 11 rows in st st.

Next row: (RS) With B, k9, mb in A, k21, mb in C, k21, mb in D, k21, mb in E, k21, mb in A, k21, mb in C, k21, mb in D, k10.

Beg with a p row, work 7 rows in st st.

Cont in st st and stripes of 4 rows each C, E and D.

Cast off.

Make bobble (mb)

Join in required colour. Work into front and back of next st until there are 5 sts, turn. Beg with a p row, work 4 rows st st on these 5 sts.

Next row: P2tog, p1, p2tog. 3 sts.

Next row: With base colour, k3tog, then cont along row according to instructions.

Scallop edging

With 4.00mm (no. 8) crochet hook, E and RS of work facing, work 151dc along cast-on edge.

Next row: Ss in first dc, *miss 2dc, 5tr in next dc, miss 2dc, ss in next dc, rep from * to end.

Fasten off.

Rep scallop edging along cast-off edge.

End piece *(make two)*

With 4mm (no. 8) needles and C, cast on 21 sts.

K1 row and p1 row.

***Next 2 rows:** k20, turn; sl 1, p to end.

Next 2 rows: k19, turn; sl 1, p to end.

Cont in this way until foll 2 rows have been worked 'k5, turn; sl 1, p to end.'

Next row: k4, (pick up front loop of st below sl st and place on left-hand needle, k it tog tbl with next sl st) 16 times, k1.

P1 row.*

Rep from * to * 5 times more. Cast off.

Button cover *(make two)*

With 3.25mm (no. 10) needles and E, cast on 11 sts.

Next row: K to end.

Next row: P to end.

Next row: K to end, inc in first and last sts.

Next row: P to end.

Rep last 2 rows twice more.

17 sts. Beg with a k row, work 4 rows in st st.

Next row: K2tog, k to last 2 sts, k2tog.

Next row: P to end.

Rep last 2 rows twice more.11 sts. Cast off.

Making up

Sew cast-on and cast-off edges of each end piece tog. Gather up centre of each one. Cover buttons according to manufacturer's instructions and sew to centre of end pieces.

Join side edges of main piece approximately 6cm from each end. Sew zip fastener into opening. Sew in end pieces to each end of open tube formed by main piece, taking care not to catch in scallop edging. Insert cushion pad and close zip fastener.

Lots of Spots

○ Make a graphic statement to match your decor with this bright and beautiful cushion.

Measurements

Cushion is 41cm square

Materials

HOW MUCH YARN

4 x 50g balls of Patons Diploma Gold DK in A - Bright aqua (shade 6243)

1 ball in B - White (shade 6187)

NEEDLES

Pair of 4mm (no. 8) needles

ADDITIONAL ITEMS

3 flat white buttons, 4cm in diameter

41cm square cushion pad

Tension

22 sts and 30 rows measure 10cm square over st st using 4mm (no. 8) needles

IT IS ESSENTIAL TO WORK TO THE STATED TENSION TO ACHIEVE SUCCESS

Cushion cover:

With 4mm (no. 8) needles and A, cast on 90 sts and commence at lower back.

1st row: (RS) k2, *p2, k2, rep from * to end.

2nd row: p2, *k2, p2, rep from * to end.

Beg with a k row, cont in st st and work 100 rows.

FRONT

Cont in st st and patt from chart.

Read odd-numbered (RS) rows from right to left and even-numbered (WS) rows from left to right. Use a separate small ball for each area of colour, twisting yarns together on WS of work when changing colour to avoid a hole forming.

1st row: k9 A, work 1st row of chart, k9 A.

2nd row: p9 A, work 2nd row of chart, p9 A.

These 2 rows set position of chart and edge sts in st st and A. Cont as set, work 40 rows of chart 3 times – 120 rows in total.

UPPER BACK

Cont in A only and work 48 rows in st st.

1st buttonhole row: k20, cast off 4 sts, (k19 including st used to cast off, cast off 4 sts) twice, k to end.

2nd buttonhole row: p to end, casting on 4 sts over those cast off on previous row.

Rep 1st and 2nd rib rows as given for lower back.

Cast off in rib

Making up

Neatly sew in all loose ends on WS of cushion cover front. Press carefully on RS of work, using a cool iron over a dry cloth. Fold cushion cover to form a square so that the upper back section overlaps lower back section. Slipstitch overlapped section together along side edges. With RS together backstitch side seams.

Turn cover to RS through opening. Sew on buttons to correspond with buttonholes. Insert cushion pad.

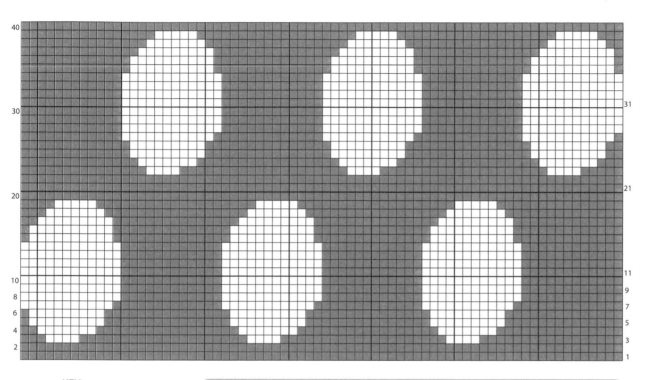

KEY
■ = A   □ = B

Reading a Chart ›››››››››››

Here is our quick and easy guide to working from a chart.

1. Each square on a chart represents a single stitch and each horizontal line a row of knitting.

2. When working from a chart, read the odd-number rows as knit rows (from right to left) and the even-numbered rows as purl rows (from left to right).

3. If you can get your chart photocopied/scanned and enlarged, you can mark your chart off as you knit with a coloured marker. You can also then write useful notes as you knit.

4. Unless specified otherwise, start knitting from the bottom right-hand corner of the chart at row 1.

Purl Stitch

1 Keep the yarn to the front of the work. Insert the right-hand needle from right to left into the front of the first stitch on the left-hand needle.

2 Use your index finger on the right hand to take the yarn that is attached to the ball over and around and under the point of the right-hand needle.

3 Draw this new loop on the right-hand needle under and through the first loop on the left-hand needle.

After you have mastered the knit stitch, the next stitch to try is purl stitch. It is the reverse of the knit stitch with the stitch formed from front to back. Again it is an important stitch and invaluable for a whole range of projects in the Big & Little Knitting Projects.

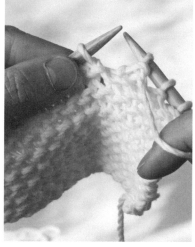

④ This forms a new stitch on the right-hand needle. At the same time, slide the original stitch off the left-hand needle.

⑤ You now have a new stitch on the right-hand needle and the yarn is still to the front of the work. You are now ready to make the next stitch by repeating these steps.

⑥ Complete the row of stitches, keeping the tension as even as possible. Now all the stitches on the left-hand needle will have been transferred to the right-hand needle. Swap the right-hand needle into your left hand and begin the next row in exactly the same way.

Rows of purl stitch will look like this (the same as rows of knit stitch) forming a garter stitch pattern with horizontal rows of interlocking stitches.

Strawberry cushion

○ Funky, bright and fun, this 3-D fruit knitted in cotton yarn and has felt 'pips' sewn on.

Measurements

Finished size approximately 40 x 40cm when stuffed

Materials

HOW MUCH YARN

4 x 50g balls of Debbie Bliss Cotton DK in colour A – Red (shade 47)

1 ball in colour B – Avocado (shade 20)

NEEDLES

Pair of 4mm (no. 8) needles

ADDITIONAL ITEMS

A4 sheet of white felt

White sewing thread and needle

Washable polyester toy stuffing

Tension

20 sts and 28 rows measure 10cm square over st st on 4mm (no. 8) needles

IT IS ESSENTIAL TO WORK TO THE STATED TENSION TO ACHIEVE SUCCESS

Note: Use a set of four double-pointed 4mm needles as st holders for leaves. They are exactly the right size and sts can easily be knitted off them on next row.

Cushion Front

With 4mm (no. 8) needles and A, cast on 10 sts.

1st row: (RS) K to end.

2nd row: P into front and back of first st, p to last st, p into front and back of last st. 1 st inc at each end of row.

3rd row: K into front and back of first st, k to last st, k into front and back of last st. 1 st inc at each end of row.

4th row: P to end.

5th row: As 3rd row.

6th row: As 2nd row.

Rep these 6 rows until there are 50 sts.

Now inc 1 st at each end of every row until there are 60 sts. P 1 row.

Inc 1 st at each end of next and 2 foll alt rows, then at each end of 2 foll 4th rows. 70 sts.

Work 21 rows straight, ending with a p row.

Next row: (RS) K2tog, k to last 2 sts, k2tog. 1 st dec at each end of row.

Cont to dec 1 st in this way at each end of 2 foll 4th rows, then at each end of next 3 alt rows. 58 sts.

Cast off 3 sts at beg of next 4 rows. 46 sts. Cast off 4 sts at beg of foll 10 rows. Cast off rem 6 sts.

Cushion Back

Work as given for Front.

Leaves and stalk

LEAVES (make four)

With 4mm needles and B, cast on 3 sts.

1st row: K3.

2nd row: P1, k1, p1.

3rd row: K1, (m1, k1) twice.

4th row: K2, p1, k2.

5th row: k2, m1, k1, m1, k2.

6th row: K3, p1, k3.

7th row: K3, m1, k1, m1, k3.

8th row: K4, p1, k4.

9th row: K4, m1, k1, m1, k4.

10th row: K5, p1, k5.

11th row: K5, m1, k1, m1, k5.

12th row: K6, p1, k6.

13th row: K6, m1, k1, m1, k6.

14th row: K7, p1, k7.

15th row: K15.

Rep 14th and 15th rows twice more, then work 14th row again. Cut off yarn and leave sts on a holder.

LEAF 5

Work as given for other leaves but do not cut off yarn.

STALK

1st row: K across 15 sts of 5th leaf, then across 15 sts of each of other 4 leaves in turn. 75 sts.

2nd row: K7, (p1, k14) 4 times, p1, k7.

3rd row: (K1, k2tog) twice, *k3, (k2tog, k1) 4 times, rep from * 3 times more, k3, (k2tog, k1) 3 times.

4th row: K5, p1, (k10, p1) 4 times, k5.

5th row: K1, (k2tog) twice, *k1, (k2tog) 5 times, rep from, * 3 times more, k1, (k2tog) twice, k1.

6th row: K3, p1, (k5, p1) 4 times, k3.

7th row: K1, *k2tog, k1, rep from * to end. 21 sts.

Work 11 rows straight in g st. Cut off yarn leaving a long end. Thread cut end through sts and pull up tight. Use yarn end to join stalk side seam, leaving leaf edges open.

Making up

From white felt cut 12 circles approximately 5cm in diameter. Pin 6 spots randomly to each side of cushion and slip stitch neatly in place. Place back and front of cushion with RS facing and backstitch around outer edges to join, leaving an opening at top. Turn RS out.

Fill with polyester toy stuffing, pushing it well down into base, and sew opening closed.

Place a little stuffing inside stalk and place on top of cushion with stalk over top seam. Slip stitch leaves neatly in place around outer edges.

Bright Aran

○ Packed full of complex Aran textures, this beautiful cushion matches traditional styling with bright contemporary colouring.

Measurements

Cushion measures 40cm square

Materials

HOW MUCH YARN

6 x 50g balls of Debbie Bliss Rialto Aran in Rust (shade 33)

NEEDLES

Pair of 4.5mm (no. 7) needles

Cable needle

ADDITIONAL ITEMS

40cm square cushion pad

Tension

20 sts and 28 rows measure 10cm square over double moss st on 4.5mm (no. 7) needles

IT IS ESSENTIAL TO WORK TO THE STATED TENSION TO ACHIEVE SUCCESS

Bramble stitch

(worked over 16 sts)

1st row: (RS) P16.

2nd row: K2, (p3tog, k1, p1, k1 all into next st) 3 times, k2.

3rd row: P16.

4th row: K2, (k1, p1, k1 all into next st, p3tog) 3 times, k2.

Rep these 4 rows to form patt.

Oxo cable

(worked over 6 sts)

1st row: (RS) K6.

2nd and every foll WS row: P6.

3rd row: C3B, C3F.

5th row: K6.

7th row: C3F, C3B.

8th row: P6.

Rep these 8 rows to form patt.

Simple cable

(worked over 4 sts)

1st row: (RS) K4.

2nd row: P4.

3rd row: C4F.

4th row: P4.

Rep these 4 rows to form patt.

Diamond cable

(worked over 17 sts)

1st row: (RS) P6, k2, MB, k2, p6.

2nd and every foll WS row: K the k sts and p the p sts.

3rd row: P6, MB, k3, MB, p6.

5th row: As 1st row.

7th row: P5, C3BP, k1, C3FP, p5.

9th row: P4, C3BP, k1, p1, k1, C3FP, p4.

11th row: P3, C3BP, k1, (p1, k1) twice, C3FP, p3.

13th row: P2, C3BP, k1, (p1, k1) 3 times, C3FP, p2.

15th row: P2, C3FP, p1, (k1, p1) 3 times, C3BP, p2.

17th row: P3, C3FP, p1 (k1, p1) twice, C3BP, p3.

19th row: P4, C3FP, p1, k1, p1, C3BP, p4.

21st row: P5, C3FP, p1, C3BP, p5.
22nd row: K6, p5, k6.

Rep these 22 rows to form patt.

Plaited cable

(worked over 14 sts)

1st row: (RS) (K2, p1) 4 times, k2.

2nd and every foll WS row: (P2, k1) 4 times, p2.

3rd row: K2, (p1, C5F) twice.

5th and 7th rows: As 1st row.

9th row: (C5B, p1) twice, k2.

11th row: As 1st row.

12th row: As 2nd row.

Rep these 12 rows to form patt.

Make bobble

(K1, p1, k1) all into next stitch, turn and p3, turn and k3tog.

Front

With 4.5mm (no. 7) needles cast on 104 sts.

Foundation row: (WS) *K2, (k1, p1, k1 all into next st, p3tog) 3 times*, k2, p6, k2, p4, k6, p5, k6, (p2, k1) 4 times, p2, k6, p5, k6, p4, k2, p6, rep from * to *, k2.

Now cont in patt as foll:

1st row: (RS) Work 16 sts as 1st row of Bramble stitch, work 6 sts as 1st row of Oxo cable, p2, work 4 sts as 1st row of Simple cable, work 17 sts as 1st row of Diamond cable, work 14 sts as 1st row of Plaited cable, work 17 sts as 1st row of Diamond cable, work 4 sts as 1st row of Simple cable, p2, work 6 sts as 1st row of Oxo cable, work last 16 sts as 1st row of Bramble stitch.

2nd row: Work 16 sts as 2nd row of Bramble stitch, work 6 sts as 2nd row of Oxo cable, p2, work 4 sts as 2nd row of Simple cable, work 17 sts as 2nd row of Diamond cable, work 14 sts as 2nd row of Plaited cable, work 17 sts as 2nd row of Diamond cable, work 4 sts as 2nd row of Simple cable, p2, work 6 sts as 2nd row of Oxo cable, work last 16 sts as 2nd row of Bramble stitch.

Cont in patt as now set until 22 rows of Diamond cable have been worked 5 times, then work a further 6 rows in patt. Cast off.

Back

With 4.5mm (no. 7) needles cast on 81 sts. Cont in double moss st as foll:

1st row: (RS) K1, *p1, k1, rep from * to end.

2nd row: P1, *k1, p1, rep from * to end.

3rd row: P1, *k1, p1, rep from * to end.

4th row: K1, *p1, k1, rep from * to end.

Rep these 4 rows until Back measures same as Front, ending with a WS row. Cast off.

Making up

With RS together, join cast-off edges (top) and side seams, leaving lower edge open. Turn RS out. Insert cushion pad and use mattress stitch to close lower edge.

Big Star

○ This cushion is definitely a bit rock 'n' roll and needs to be centre stage on your sofa!

Measurements
Cushion measures 45cm square

Materials
5 x 50g balls of King Cole Merino Blend DK in colour A – French Navy (shade 25)

2 balls in colour B – Aran (shade 46)

1 ball in colour C – Scarlet (shade 9)

NEEDLES
Pair of 3.75mm (no. 9) needles

ADDITIONAL ITEMS
Stitch holder

4.00mm (no. 8) crochet hook

6 buttons

45cm square cushion pad

Tension
24 sts and 32 rows measure 10cm square over st st on 3.75mm (no. 9) needles

IT IS ESSENTIAL TO WORK TO THE STATED TENSION TO ACHIEVE SUCCESS

Cushion front

With 3.75mm (no. 9) needles and A, cast on 108 sts. Beg with a k row, work 15 rows in st st. Now work side borders as foll:

1st row: (WS) P12 A, 84 B, 12 A.

2nd row: K12 A, 84 B, 12 A.

3rd row: As 1st row.

Cont in patt from chart as foll:

1st row: (RS) K12 A, 5 B, working from right to left work across 37 sts of 1st row of chart as foll: k9 B, p2 C, k26 B, then working from left to right work 1st row of chart again as foll: k26 B, p2 C, k9 B, cont to end of row as foll: k5 B, 12 A.

2nd row: P12 A, 5 B, working from right to left work across 37 sts of 2nd row of chart as foll: p9 B, k2 C, p26 B, working from left to right work 2nd row of chart again as foll: p26 B, k2 C, p9 B, cont to end of row as foll: p5 B, 12 A.

Cont in patt from chart as set, noting that background is worked in st st and star motif in reverse st st until 108th row has been completed. Cut off C.

Cont in B with side border in A as before for 3 more rows. Cut off B.

Work 15 more rows in st st with A only, ending with a WS row.

Cast off.

Cushion back

With 3.75mm (no. 9) needles and A, cast on 107 sts. Beg with a p row, work 7 rows in st st.

DIVIDE FOR OPENING

1st row: (RS) K58, turn and cont on this group of sts for first side of opening.

2nd row: K9, p to end.

3rd row: K58.

4th–12th rows: Rep 2nd and 3rd rows 4 times, then work 2nd row again.

13th row: K52, cast off next 3 sts, k to end.

14th row: K3, cast on 3 sts, k3, p to end.

15th row: K58.

16th row: K9, p to end.

17th–32nd rows: Rep 15th and 16th rows 8 times more.

Rep 13th–32nd rows 4 times more, then work 13th and 14th rows again (6 buttonholes worked in all).

Now rep 15th and 16th rows 6 times, then work 15th row again. Cut off yarn and leave these 58 sts on a holder.

With A, cast 9 sts for button flap on to needle holding 49 sts at base of opening, k across cast-on sts, then k across rem 49 sts. 58 sts. Keeping 9 sts at inner edge in g st, work 125 rows in st st, ending with a WS row.

Next row: Cast off 9 sts, k to end. 49 sts.

Next row: P49, then work across sts on holder as foll: k9, p49. 107 sts.

Beg with a k row, work 7 rows in st st. Cast off.

Working from chart

When working from chart, use a separate ball of yarn for each area of colour, twisting yarns together on WS of work when changing colour to avoid holes forming. When working star motif, twist C on WS of back where appropriate, bringing it to back and front of work as necessary to work stitches.

Making up

Press according to directions on ball band.

Using B double, join to back of work at inner point of one of star 'arms'. With 4.00mm (no. 8) hook, work a row of double crochet around star outline to neaten.

Sew down button flap to upper and lower edge of buttonhole flap. Place cushion front and back with RS facing and join side seams. Turn RS out through back opening. Sew on buttons and insert cushion pad.

☐ = B
■ = C

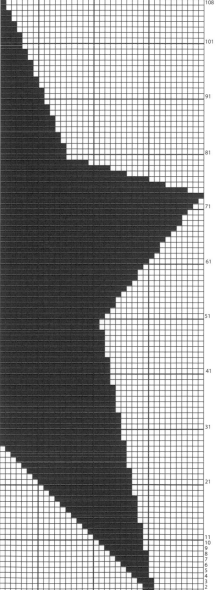

Repairing a Dropped Stitch

The first thing to do is to secure the dropped stitch to prevent any further damage. To do this, work the tip of a safety pin into the head of the dropped stitch and then fasten the pin so that the stitch cannot slip down any further. Now follow steps 1 - 8 to repair the dropped stitch.

1 With the right side facing you, knit to where the dropped stitch is and remove the pin. The horizontal bars of the stitches will look like a ladder above the dropped stitch.

2 Keeping the needles gently apart, place a small crochet hook through the loop of the dropped stitch from front to back.

3 Take the crochet hook under the first horizontal bar.

4 Carefully draw the hook back through the loop of the stitch, bringing the yarn that forms the horizontal bar with it.

It is inevitable that you will drop a stitch at some time when you are knitting, but it can be picked up and the knitting repaired. All you need for the task is a small crochet hook.

⑤ Pull the horizontal bar through the loop so it forms the next loop. You have now picked the stitch up from the first row where it was dropped.

⑥ Continue working up the bars of the ladder, repeating steps 2-5 until you reach the current row of knitting.

⑦ Place the final loop back onto the left-hand needle, using the crochet hook to slip it so that the needle goes through the loop from left to right, the same as the other stitches.

⑧ Knit the dropped stitch as normal and carry on to the end of the row. Your knitting should now be returned to its perfect state.

Your Chunky Throw

○ Get started on your gorgeous chunky knit throw with this easy moss stitch square.

Double Moss Stitch Square

Double Moss Stitch Square

Measurements

Finished square 20 x 20cm

Materials

Ball of cream yarn provided
(save any leftover yarn)

Pair of 10mm needles (no. 000)
provided

Tension

9 sts and 11 rows measure 10cm
square over patt.

IT IS ESSENTIAL TO WORK TO THE
STATED TENSION TO ACHIEVE
SUCCESS

What to do

With 10mm (no. 000) needles
and cream yarn, cast on 18 sts.

K 2 rows.

1st row: K2, (p1, k1) 7 times, k2.

2nd row: K2, (k1, p1) 7 times, k2.

3rd row: As 2nd row.

4th row: As 1st row.

Rep these 4 rows 3 more times,
then 1st and 2nd rows again.

K 3 rows.

Cast off purlwise